DOGS

DOGS

A PHILOSOPHICAL GUIDE
TO OUR BEST FRIENDS

MARK ALIZART

TRANSLATED BY
ROBIN MACKAY

polity

First published in French © Presses Universitaires de France/Humensis, *Chiens*, 2018

This English edition © Polity Press, 2020

Polity Press
65 Bridge Street
Cambridge CB2 1UR, UK

Polity Press
101 Station Landing
Suite 300
Medford, MA 02155, USA

ISBN-13: 978-1-5095-3728-0

A catalogue record for this book is available from the British Library.

Library of Congress Cataloging-in-Publication Data

Names: Alizart, Mark, author.
Title: Dogs / Mark Alizart.
Other titles: Chiens. English
Description: Medford, MA : Polity 2019. | Includes bibliographical
    references and index.
Identifiers: LCCN 2019020140 (print) | LCCN 2019981071 (ebook) | ISBN
    9781509537280 (hardback) | ISBN 9781509537303 (epub)
Subjects: LCSH: Dogs--Anecdotes.
Classification: LCC SF426.2 .A4513 2019 (print) | LCC SF426.2 (ebook) |
    DDC 636.7--dc23
LC record available at https://lccn.loc.gov/2019020140
LC ebook record available at https://lccn.loc.gov/2019981071

Typeset in 12.5 on 16.5 pt Perpetua
by Fakenham Prepress Solutions, Fakenham, Norfolk NR21 8NL
Printed and bound in Great Britain by TJ International Limited

For further information on Polity, visit our website:
politybooks.com

Contents

CONTENTS

For Brune
In memory of Luther

ACKNOWLEDGEMENTS

Luther (†), Eckhart, Ayrton, Barthes, Holy, Igloo, Lilou, Papi, Koshka, Max (†), Brutus (†), Human, Tobias and Otto (†), Okra, Milk (†) and all the others. As well as Martin Bethenod, Marianne Alphant, and Thomas Lepeltier for their invaluable readings of the text, Laurent de Sutter for his trust, Brune Compagnon-Janin and Suzanne Alizart. Not forgetting Marion Ivy, the Association Celtiques Lévriers I got my beloved dog from, and all those who help abandoned dogs to (re)discover joy in the company of their fellow humans.

THE JOY OF DOGS

One day, dogs will rule the earth.

At least this was the idea that occurred to an American science fiction writer in the aftermath of the Second World War. In Clifford Simak's novel *City*, after humankind is annihilated by one too many wars, only animals remain, and dogs in particular undergo a remarkable transformation: over time they stop eating meat, learn to talk, and eventually surpass their former masters in intelligence – so much so that, over thousands of years, they restore order to the planet, establishing a peaceful and harmonious government.

Simak's futuristic hypothesis may strike some as rather surprising. Not so much the idea of the end of humanity

— something with which we are, alas, all too familiar — as the idea that it is dogs that will replace us. If we had to choose an animal (rather than a cyborg) to replace humans, we would usually think of apes as better placed in the order of succession, as suggested in *Planet of the Apes*. But anyone who really loves dogs will understand Simak's choice. For dogs have at least two qualities that make them very well suited to the job.

The first is a startling resilience in the face of hardship that could prove invaluable in a post-apocalyptic era: dogs know how to live on scraps, and even on scraps of scraps; they will sleep anywhere and anyhow; they can adapt to any environment; and they are capable of overcoming nearly any kind of pain. This first character trait has no doubt been shaped over millions of years of evolution. After all, when we talk about a 'dog's life', we don't mean an idyllic existence. A 'dog of a day' is not a great day. 'To die like a dog' is a nasty way to go. Dogs have grown up the hard way, far away from the wolf pack. They have had to learn to live a life of vagrancy and opportunistic plunder. Later on, coming into contact with the first human encampments, they were driven away (or sometimes eaten) like the unwholesome rovers they seemed to be. But then they discovered something even more ferocious than enemies – *masters*: they were imprisoned, trained, and beaten. And yet, at each stage, they got up again and carried on.

But it is a second quality that makes them truly suited to replace us, one that is almost the opposite of the first: their extraordinary sensitivity, without which their strength would be nothing but brutality. Dogs are naturally gentle with children, patient with adults, fraternal with other animals; in short, they seem to possess true wisdom and would be capable of expressing it if only they could talk, as the saying goes. Dogs haven't just gritted their teeth and swallowed all the humiliations that evolution has served up to them. Unlike other animals in the same situation, they have not become hardened, or even ugly, as have the hyena, the vulture, and the rat among wild beasts. And, unlike circus animals forcibly domesticated by humans, they have not turned melancholy or gone mad. On the contrary, dogs seem to have grown gentler. They have met their fate with a certain nonchalance, a kind of joy even. The dog meets everyone and everything with that phlegmatic attitude marvellously expressed in Droopy's celebrated catchphrase – which is no less profound than

Bartleby's: 'You know what? I'm happy.' Of course there are unhappy dogs, neurotic dogs, and timorous dogs. But they're usually animals that have been ill-treated. A dog needs only find a good master and it will invariably gravitate toward joy just as surely as a sunflower turns to face the sun.

Dogs genuinely seem to have become 'philosophers', if we accept the idea of the Stoics, the Buddhists, and Spinoza that wisdom consists in accommodating oneself, with simplicity and gratitude, to what life has to offer.

The following pages are devoted to understanding this miracle, the miracle of the joy of dogs; to understanding it and, if at all possible, to learning from it for ourselves – as all indications seem to suggest that Simak was right to fear the worst for humankind and that we ourselves may soon have to learn to live 'like dogs' upon an earth devastated by our own madness.

THE SHAME OF THE ANIMAL KINGDOM

It is a cruel paradox that, whilst we all seek joy, whenever we meet a person who is truly joyful, we suspect that she must be either stupid or crazy. For how could one be truly happy in this vale of tears? Wouldn't you have to be completely ignorant about life or, worse, a little mean, to be happy about all the misery that surrounds us?

Zen monks seem to have got used to being seen as eccentrics. According to an ancient koan, when you asked the venerable Ma-Tsou 'show me what wisdom is', he tweaked your nose. At least he didn't get bothered that way. Dogs aren't so lucky. Despite the exceptional qualities they are renowned for – such as helping shepherds, or hunting, guiding blind people, smelling diseases even – they are subject to extraordinary injustices. Whether it's Dingo, Pluto, Scooby Doo, or Santa's Little Helper, our dogs are often unfairly referred to as cowards, clumsy, clowns, not to say imbeciles (Stupid is even the name John Fante gives to the dog in his eponymous novella, albeit lovingly).

There is no 'dog in boots'. It is Reynard the Fox who appears in a fable that extols animal intelligence, and in the modern fairy tales of Disney cartoons it's a mouse, Mickey. The marvellous animals in Lewis Carroll's *Alice's Adventures in Wonderland* are the mysterious Cheshire Cat and the March Hare, not the common dog; in *The Jungle Book* the Serpent Kaa and the panther Bagheera, but not the dog. In the Bible, the lion, the ox, and the eagle are the animals that represent the Apostles — not the dog. The French have their Gallic rooster, the Russians their bear, the Americans their bald eagle — but no country has a dog as its national symbol. Even the English, with their Churchillian bulldog and the Queen's corgis at hand, gave preference to the lion, although no lion has ever walked the soil of Albion ...

There are exceptions. Rin Tin Tin, Lassie, and Tintin's Snowy all seem like persistent and heroic characters.

But are they really? Is their unfaltering faithfulness anything more than blind obedience? We can hardly praise them for it, any more than we can praise watchdogs trained by drug dealers to defend them against the police, or White Dog in Romain Gary's eponymous novel for attacking black people on sight. In fact, these sanctimonious stereotypes can even render dogs positively irritating. Up to a point, the imbecile may invite leniency and compassion, but anyone so desperate to please is just asking for rejection. Worse, if it turns out that dogs aren't stupid, then we can only imagine that they must be slackers and cowards. For Jean de La Fontaine, the moral of the fable 'The Wolf and the Dog' is that the dog is not idiotic but contemptible. The dog has deliberately renounced his freedom, selling it for a mess of pottage. Unable to fight for its share of the kill, it has had to get used to begging for it instead.

And there is an even worse accusation: the dog is not just cowardly, it is vicious. It actually enjoys being dominated, takes pleasure in it. It genuinely likes eating repugnant stuff and sniffing filthy smells. Why else is the word 'dog' an insult in almost all cultures? It was once common practice to name a dog Rex or Prince. During the nineteenth century, Bismarck was a popular name for dogs in France. Before that, many dogs were called Turk. Such names were rarely given in homage, but more often to humiliate the powerful, to bring them down and put them on all fours. Donald Trump, the first president of the United States not to own a dog, knows something about this, since he calls all of his political adversaries 'dogs'.

The fact that women are often called 'bitches' from the moment they manifest any kind of sexual desire comes from the same source. In the male imaginary women must enjoy being 'dominated' just as dogs do. 'Bitch', 'woman', 'homosexual' and 'foreigner' are all words used interchangeably to designate those beings who have been humiliated and rendered invisible by phallocratic civilisations unable to understand that the values of freedom and dignity may not belong in principle to the male sex in its erectile form.

Unfortunately, although reparations are finally under way to restore the formerly 'dominated' to their rightful place, it does not seem that the dog will ever be afforded the same consideration. For the dog has perhaps one additional failing. Dogs never ask for any redress. They *truly* love the patriarchal order. Like those unfortunate women in the 1950s who agreed with their husband that they shouldn't be given the right to vote, or like those alienated workers who vote billionaires into government in the honest belief they will defend their interests, the dog belongs to that negative faction that seems fated always to spoil things for the wider minority. Indeed, the dog is such a complex case in our culture that sometimes it puts off even defenders committed to the cause of animal liberation.

Obviously, all animal rights supporters agree that dogs should be protected against mistreatment; the *Brown Dog*, a statue erected in London in the twentieth century in honour of a canine victim of unnecessary medical experiments, bears historical witness to this cause. But when it comes to knowing how to treat dogs 'well', divisions emerge. According to some, the abandonment of dogs should be severely punished, since evidence suggests that a lone dog is condemned to a life of misery. But others believe – and anarchists such as Élisée Reclus and Bakunin already suggested this – that dogs should be 'liberated' from their masters and delivered back into the wild, even if this is, in some sense, against their own will.

In his *Abécédaire*, Gilles Deleuze, who was a great friend of animals, clearly indicates that dogs do not deserve the same respect as the other beasts that roam his writings, from splendid wolf packs to Jakob von Uexküll's humble tick. The dog's bark, he says, is 'the shame of the animal kingdom'. What better way to say that, even if (according to Deleuze) every man needs to experience a 'becoming-animal, a becoming-woman, a becoming-minor', the dog is too much of a minority within the animal kingdom for us to lower ourselves to its level? And yet, in this expression of a feeling of 'shame', how can one not sense what it is that brings us close to dogs?

Shame is a very specific emotion. We do not feel it in relation to any animal other than the dog, for shame presupposes empathy and identification. To have a dog, to love a dog, and to love it precisely for all the reasons that make us ashamed is in fact equivalent to loving the dark part of ourselves, to making peace with it – precisely to overcoming shame, and therefore overcoming the self-hatred that shame involves. And that would be true wisdom, yes – and perhaps true joy. So much so that it might be better to say, against Deleuze or right beside him, that it is only by experiencing a becoming-dog that one can truly experience becoming-human.

CANIS MAJOR

All profound joys are scandalous, because, as Georges Bataille said of eroticism, joy assents to life even in death. And so does the joy of dogs, which is definitely on the side of violence and sexuality. Their wisdom truly deserves the name because it embraces death and (re) generation, stimulates fear, and mobilises the powers of the unconscious.

Our ancestors seem to have known this better than we do, fortunately. In ancient times dogs were an object of veneration, and some were even elevated to godliness. We see this first and foremost in the most ancient symbol of the dog, Sirius, the brightest star in the Milky Way and the one whose appearance announces the great droughts of summer.

For tens of millions of years the sky has offered humanity an extraordinary spectacle: the 'Greater Dog', Canis Major, rising above the horizon at the end of what is now the month of July, at the feet of an immense hunter, the constellation of Orion. Just in front of them, a 'Hare', Lepus, scurries away and a 'Dove', Columba, flies off. Above them, a puppy, Canis Minor, the 'Lesser Dog', looks on, yapping. Opposite them, a gigantic 'Bull', Taurus, begins its charge, its eye the fiery red star Aldebaran.

It is impossible to overstate the impression this nocturnal spectacle must have made upon its first witnesses. Most cave paintings and mythological tales are attempts to 'explain' the celestial vault. Many animals are represented in a circle on cave ceilings, sometimes in the same order as the constellations; among them there are dogs alongside an archer much like Orion, which confirms that the dog was already 'man's best friend' from very early times.

The battles between Achaeans and Trojans in the *Iliad* are battles between constellations. The hierarchy of warriors mirrors that of the stars: Achilles, the greatest warrior of Greek antiquity, is also associated with Sirius, the brightest of the stars. Thus he is described in *Iliad* 22 as 'Orion's dog', but also as an 'unwelcome sign', which 'brings much fever upon the wretched mortals' (lines 29–30). Pseudo-Eratosthenes' *Katasterimoi* (*Placements among the Stars*) tells us that in Greek *seirios* (σείριος) means 'ardent' and 'burning' and states that the real name of Canis Major, the name given it by Hephaestus, god of the forge and its first master, was 'Fireball' (Laelaps, from λαῖλαψ). For the ancient Greeks, the dog, or rather the bitch, was always 'on heat'.

The Dog Star, which the Romans called Canicula, 'Lesser Dog', has become synonymous with intense heat. In his *Natural History* Pliny the Elder writes: 'Who does not know that the rising of the Dog Star kindles the ardour of the sun? The most powerful effects are felt on earth from this star: when it rises, the seas are troubled, the wines in our cellar ferment, and stagnant waters are set in motion' (Book 2, ch. 40). Canicula was also supposed to have an analogous effect on dogs: 'Dogs, during the whole of this period, also are peculiarly disposed to become rabid' (ibid.). Actaeon is devoured by one of his own dogs during such an episode, but only because he has become rabid – sexually rabid this time – with desire for Artemis,

14

herself indiscriminately associated with the bitch and the bear.

Another book of the greatest importance is set in motion by the Dog Star: the *Mahabharata*. At the beginning of this most sacred of Indian tales, princes beat a puppy, which turns out to belong to Sarama, the great canine goddess Canis Major. She then demands vengeance for Canis Minor, thus initiating the cycle of wars that the book goes on to narrate. Inversely, the *Mahabharata* ends when a dog finally receives justice. The very end of the book tells of how Yudhisthira, king of kings, on the brink of death, refuses to climb into the chariot of the god Indra that will take him to the heavens, unless he can bring along his mangy dog, who has accompanied him throughout the latter years of his life. When Indra tells him that this is impossible, Yudhisthira is ready to renounce paradise; but it then turns out that the dog in question was the embodiment of Dharma, the god of gods, who took that form so as to test the purity of the king's soul. Having passed the test, the king of kings is granted eternal life and the book can come to a close.

Twixt Dog and Wolf

A figure of the Last Judgment in ancient Egypt, Anubis is a dog carrying a set of scales. He weighs the souls of the dead. Stationed at the beginning and the end of one's life, he is the god who embalms deceased Pharaohs and is responsible for accompanying their soul to the final resting place. Anubis, whose Egyptian name is Inpu, is related to Isis, goddess of the underworld, whom the Egyptians also associated with Sirius and Canis Major. Similarly, Kala Bhairava, the Hindu god of time, master of clocks and of death, is always represented with a dog at his feet. And, according to the ancient Greeks, the gates of the underworld are guarded by Cerberus, a multiheaded mastiff who watches over Persephone, goddess of death and of springtime's return.

Some say that this representation of dogs alongside psychopomp divinities is explained by their love of carrion. But Xolotl, the dog god of the Aztec religion, tells us otherwise. Although the Xoloitzcuintli – the hairless black breed that inspired him – looks somewhat like a hyena, its liturgical role is not just to lead human souls to Mictlan, the kingdom of shadows; Xolotl is also the god who accompanies the sun into darkness and the protector of twins and twinning. In other words, rather than just being a god of death, the dog god Xolotl is the god who ensures the passage between the opposite or symmetrical polarities – the twins – of life and death, night and day. And for good reason: the *dialectical* nature of dogs had not escaped the notice of the ancients: a dog is half savage and half civilised, with a foot in each world, stationed at their exact meeting place. The dog is a go-between, a messenger – like Hermanubis, the syncretic god found in certain temples in Alexandria, who has the head of Anubis and the body of Hermes, the Greek messenger god.

According to Hesiod, Cerberus is also *double* in the following sense: he has a two-headed brother, Orthos. Now, the ancient Greek name Cerberus (Κέρβερος), of unknown etymology, has been poetically associated with a Sanskrit adjective meaning 'spotted', 'speckled' – which would make Cerberus 'the Spotted'; and *orthos* (ὀρθός) meant 'plain', which would make Orthos 'the Plain' or 'the Straight'. Together, then, they form a fundamental couple: the one and the multiple. In China and Japan, Buddhist and Shinto temples are traditionally guarded by two dogs, also twins: the Komainu (literally 'Korean Dogs'). One has its mouth open, indicating that it is pronouncing the vowel 'a'; the other has its mouth closed, as if to say 'um'. Together they pronounce *aum*, the sacred syllable and mantra of Buddhist monks, the primordial sound of the universe. In other words, the Komainu, together, form the alpha and omega of the world, bookending the beginning and the end of times. The Komainu also exhibit the *internal* duality of the dog that we have already seen in Sirius–Canicula: according to many, these dogs are lions (*shi*), and dogs and lions express the two polarities, *yin* and *yang*, of the same animal. A Buddhist legend tells of how Siddhartha was always accompanied by a shih tzu that could transform itself into a 'snow lion', a wild and untamed creature, at any sign of danger (the same lion that would become the emblem of Tibet). Conversely, another Chinese legend has it that agriculture (and thus civilisation) was brought to humans by a lost dog who transported grains in his coat.

While today we might think of domestication as a diminution for which the dog's only possible excuse is idiocy, cowardliness or vice, our ancestors understood domestication as an augmentation of being, and even as the true source of canine wisdom. In their eyes, the dog was not a denatured animal but an unclassifiable or, rather, a *transclass* one – an animal that was not subject to the separations that limit ordinary beings. It was to be treated with great respect, like the *hijras*, Indian transgender people, because, since it knew the path that ran from one cosmic polarity to another, in some sense the dog watched over the balance of the world. Were this balance to be disturbed, savagery would threaten to spread like wildfire throughout civilisation.

Sola Fido

Almost nothing remains of the great canine myths of antiquity in our contemporary representation of dogs, apart from the idea that dogs can sense when their master is about to die, and then the panicked newspaper headlines that we can rely on to appear at least once a year, like a distant echo of the legend of Actaeon: 'Mad Dog Eats Owner'.

For one, dogs have changed a great deal since antiquity – they have ceased to be wild, dangerous in nature, flea-infested, foaming at the mouth, or specially bred monsters such as the dogs of war, those 'protector dogs' (the breed now known as Cane Corso) unleashed to assault the enemy frontline, dogs that would rip a boar to pieces with only a flash of the fangs. And we ourselves have changed. Our relation to the stars, to death, and to nature has been profoundly transformed. In particular, monotheism has come between the religions of antiquity and ourselves. And it is monotheism that has now taken control of those *thresholds* and *passages* that were once the preserve of the dog. Saint Peter has replaced Cerberus at the gates of Tartarus. The one God has become the only being capable of moving between worlds, after the image of Jesus descending into hell.

Abraham has to submit to God in order to obtain his blessing. Christians must submit to Christ in order to secure their salvation. Muslims must submit to Allah in order to enjoy eternal life. Whereas pagan lore is full of humans who prove to be craftier than the gods, the one God leaves the believer with no margin whatsoever for manoeuvre: the believer has to obey God *just as a dog obeys its master*. What better way to say that monotheism, in taking over from the canine myths, also made religion into an enterprise of domestication?

Our modern love–hate relationship with our dogs has no other origin than this mimetic, triangular rivalry established from Judaism onward between dog, human, and God. The human has become a dog before God, so that dogs in their turn have become little humans before us. What God is to humans – a master – we have become for dogs, and, inversely, what the human is to God – a servant – the dog has become for us. We have begun to adore the dog the way we would like to be loved by God, we have begun to treat it as another version of us because we have recognised that it is made in our image. The essential quality we attribute to dogs in the current epoch proves this: we do not see them as dual, complex, transgender, or transclass, but as 'faithful'. The dog becomes Fido because humans wants to show their love for God by attesting to their faith (*fides*) in him.

It is precisely with monotheism that there appears the modern figure of the dog as a 'happy imbecile', a figure directly inspired by the grace we attribute to those who are 'simple in spirit' and who place obedience above disputation; a figure inspired by the idea that 'the Lord rewards the innocent'.

Martin Luther himself is proof of this: he owned a tiny little Pomeranian (a spitz) that he chose to baptise Tölpel, that is, Goofy – 'clumsy' or 'silly' in German (Luther also called him sometimes Helferlein, his 'little assistant'). This nickname didn't mean that he didn't love the little dog, of course, quite the contrary, but he loved it in a modern way, not as the former demigod of transit. Luther was a great dog lover; we even attribute to him three sayings about dogs that are quite remarkable, given the theological rigour with which he execrated almost everything that didn't fit with his conception of Christianity. The first is that the dog is God's most precious gift to us, and would be recognised as such were the species not so common. The second is that the dog is a model of faith for the Christian. And the third is that dogs will go to heaven.

Prior to the reformer, one of the blessed, the Dominican friar Henry Suso, owed his revelation to a dog. As he carved Jesus's name into his chest with a knife, in order to make himself worthy of His mercy, Suso saw a puppy playing with a dirty foot-cloth. Struck by the dog's simple joy in amusing itself with such a lowly object, he understood that redemption is granted only to those who have grace and simplicity – in other words, he saw that by mortifying his flesh he was only glorifying himself, and that in doing so he was distancing himself from redemption. He decided instead to love God like a little dog, in constant celebration of the world.

In Christian painting, little 'lapdogs' on the Lutheran model appear almost everywhere from the fifteenth century on, very different from their psychopomp ancestors, who were either on heat or rabid. Tiny spitzes, Schnauzers and poodles featured in domestic scenes – at the feet of the Arnolfinis, for example, symbolising fidelity between husband and wife, or a few metres from Saint Augustine in a painting by Carpaccio, symbolising fidelity between man and god – but also in paintings on religious themes, alongside saints, and even with Christ. In Albrecht Dürer's work the dog is almost a signature. There are Portuguese waterdogs in his *Flagellation* and in many plates of his *Apocalypse with Pictures*, each one sporting a 'lion cut' (being shaved, apart from the head), to evoke the royalty of Jesus. At the feet of Dürer's *Saint Jerome* lies a German spitz, once again alongside a lion. In *Saint Eustachius* and in *Knight, Death and the Devil*, Pointers scurry hither and thither. Dürer also made many portrait engravings of dogs, almost always Hungarian Greyhounds (the Magyar Agár breed), the same dog that sleeps alongside his angel of melancholy. One possible reason for this obsession was that Dürer, Hungarian or 'Magyar' by birth, self-represented himself as a Magyar Agár.

At this point in history, astrologers no longer identify the dog with Sirius; they link it instead to Saturn. It is no longer an incarnation of rage but of the internal contemplative life. The frontispiece of Robert Burton's *Anatomy of Melancholy* features a Greyhound in the section illustrating 'Solitude', as if, deprived of the raison d'être with which pagan antiquity had endowed it, the dog had become a wandering soul, having lost even its legendary joy. In Velázquez's *Las Meninas*, the German Shepherd is deep in sleep, absent from the scene, so that one of the king's fools has to give him a kick to wake him as the monarch enters.

Alas, with monotheism there also appears the suspicion that dogs may be not only simple spirits, but evil ones. The 'bad dog' is a scapedog. It's the dog we beat when we come home from work after having been beaten down by our own boss. It's the dog we get angry with because it dares to defy us in ways we dare not defy our own master. It's the dog we punish out of jealousy, because it is more holy than we ourselves are. In short, it's the dog we humiliate because we ourselves feel humiliated at being God's little bow-wow. It is here that we find another reason for our scorn for dogs; but this scorn is entirely our problem, it is the fruit of the hatred and frustration we feel – but cannot allow ourselves to express – at all the vexations imposed upon us by the religion of the one true God. The more we bow down before God, the more we submit to him, the more pious we are – in short, the more we ourselves are good dogs, on all fours before him – the more we detest being like this and the more we hate dogs, who present to us too faithful a mirror of what we ourselves are. Dogs are subjected to our inner anger with ourselves for not being able to be better humans. They have to be removed from our sight so that no one, ever, may be able to insult us by comparing us with them.

THE DOG VINCI CODE

Luckily, dogs can't be got rid of quite so easily. Dogs have survived everything life has thrown at them, and for thousands of years. So it should come as no surprise that they have also managed to survive monotheism. Indeed, it's fascinating to see how, in spite of everything that religions of the one God have done to erase the ancient dog, it has continually discovered ways to invite itself back into our lives again.

I said earlier that there were no dogs in the Bible, except where the term was used as an insult. But this is not entirely true. On one unique but magnificent occasion, they are cast in a favourable light, reminiscent of antiquity, in a story that tells us a great deal about the cynegetic origin of monotheism. The scene takes place in the seventh verse of chapter 11 of Exodus. When the pharaoh's slaves, who will become the people of Israel, flee from Egypt, they come across a pack of dogs. If the dogs bark, the militia will discover and capture them. If the dogs are quiet, they will be saved. Now, the dogs are 'struck by a light in the middle of the night', as Emmanuel Levinas says in his lengthy commentary on this passage. 'Not a dog shall growl', says the Book. In other words, dogs chose to lay down before the prophets of the new God and testify on their behalf precisely by not testifying to their presence.

Here Judaism seems to recognise that in a certain sense the powers it attributes to itself are those of the ancient dog – to the point where one might ask whether it did not in fact achieve its ascendency by absorbing the ancient cult of the dog wholesale, whether it did not triumph over paganism simply by taking its place. After all, the Hebrews came out of Egypt and could well have brought with them the idea of the one God (Aten–Adonai), and therefore everything that comes along with it, Isis and Anubis in particular. Samuel Joseph Agnon, one of whose novels features a canine protagonist named Balak – literally 'he who licks the blood of Israel' – suggested that, in recognition of this act, the dog deserved to be adopted as the emblem of the Jewish people. That would have made it the only nation with such an emblem. Although this did not come to pass, when Jews celebrate Exodus, at Passover, they are perhaps still paying unconscious tribute to the dog, since Passover means 'passage': it is the festival of go-between gods, and therefore of dogs.

In Islam, which has an undeserved reputation for unkindness to dogs, we find another trace of this legend, which is also a manifestation of Islam's unavowed relation to Judaism. One of the suras of the Koran, the Seven Sleepers of Ephesus, which is evidently inspired by Exodus, recounts how seven devout young men on the run from a militia took refuge in a cave. As they were followed by a dog, Kitmir ('Spotty') – probably a Saluki, a breed that Mohammad owned and that is still much loved in the Middle East – they feared they would be given away by its barking, but instead Kitmir began to speak, pledging his loyalty to them. Under his watchful eye the young men fell asleep, only to awaken three hundred lunar years later, safe and sound, still guarded by the dog – who, tradition has it, went to paradise.

In a popular legend of medieval Christianity another ancient dog can be glimpsed, in the shape of Saint Christopher. The story goes that, once upon a time, there existed men with dog's heads, *cynocephali*, a source of terror for all around them. One, who lived in Lycia (home of those wild dogs of the species *Lycaon pictus*), was nicknamed 'the Reprobate'. He sought to enter into the service of the most powerful master possible. One day, however, he met Jesus. Jesus was not afraid of him, even asked him for help in crossing a river. Recognising in Jesus a very powerful being since he showed no fear in spite of Reprobate's monstrosity, the latter took Jesus upon his back – an act that earned him the name Christopher (*Christo-phoros*, 'bearer of Christ', from χριστός 'anointed' and φέρειν 'to carry, bear' in Greek); he also received human form in exchange – by which we should perhaps understand, rather, that he received *canine form*, in the sense that, like all myths, the legend of Saint Christopher seeks to explain an enigma: that of having seen how jackals can become true dogs, how dangerous wild animals can become affectionate and obliging companion animals.

This legend, which explains why Saint Christopher is represented with a dog's head in some very old churches, especially Orthodox ones, also brings to mind the story of Saint John the Baptist. Christopher enables Jesus to cross a river just as John baptises Jesus in a river, and just as Anubis purifies souls in water – water that symbolises the crossing over into death. John is decapitated; Anubis loses his head, which is replaced by that of a jackal. John is associated with the summer solstice; Anubis is Canicula, the Dog Star. It is possible, then, that Anubis, John and Christopher are one and the same. Just as John and Christopher herald Christ, Anubis heralds Jesus. And, of course, Jesus is joyous. Jesus is joy personified. Christ is that nocturnal sun formerly known as Sirius, the fearsome incandescent star. Christ is, precisely, Rex – just like the dog. The 'king of the Jews' ensures communication between earth and heaven, life and death; he is a distant cousin of the great thanatological dogs. Indeed, at Easter, which is the Christian version of Passover, he is surrounded by a dove and a hare, Columba and Lepus, the two constellations that surround Canis Major.

Other stories tend to marry Christian and Pagan themes. In the 1250s a greyhound was canonised by some villagers in the diocese of Lyon under the name

Saint Guinefort. In the *Divine Comedy* Dante repeats a popular legend that may have been inspired by this episode: Canto 1 of *Inferno* tells of how a greyhound will free humanity after having punished a she-wolf. The hidden meaning of such a prophecy cannot have been too much of a mystery at the time: the she-wolf was the symbol of Rome, the papal city corrupted by vice, the 'whore of Babylon'; and the greyhound, with which Dante associates the numerical value 515 – DXV in Roman numerals – is therefore a DVX (*dux*, 'leader'): a DUKE or a providential prince charged with subduing it (*dux* evokes *rex*).

One other great Christian equally relied on his association with the dog: Saint Dominic. His mother had dreamt that she would give birth to a black-and-white dog with a torch in its muzzle that would bring light to the world; and so Dominic decided that he would cast himself in the image of a dog that embraced the world of truth. The Dominican order he went on to found must therefore be understood as the order of *Domini canes*, the 'dogs of God'. Often represented in paintings with a star on his forehead, probably an allusion to Sirius, Dominic stands midway between the mysteries of Egypt and Christianity.

One can find even a great astral dog hidden in the depths of the evangelical tradition – a cosmic and sexual she-dog from the prehistory of humanity. To the right of the head of Christ on the tympanum of Vézelay Abbey, which was built in the twelfth century, two dogs can be seen biting their own tails, just like Ourobouros the serpent. They represent the month of July, Canicula, in the great zodiac that frames the scene. But, since July 22nd, the first day of Canicula, is also the feast day of Saint Mary Magdalene, to whom Vézelay is consecrated, it is difficult not to think that they also represent her – especially in a place like this, where they can be seen by all, carved out as they are at the very centre of the cornerstone of the entire edifice, almost supporting it. Are these intertwined dogs Canis Major, the sacred woman and prostitute with whom Mary Magdalene would (incorrectly, but that's another story) be associated throughout the Middle Ages?

Other sources may perhaps support this reading. In his representation of the Last Supper, Veronese represented a Pointer in the foreground, to the left of Christ, as if that dog were the subject of the painting. Scandalised, the Inquisition ordered him to replace it – with Mary Magdalene ... Veronese refused, but was forced to rename his painting *The Feast in the House of Levi*. Similarly, in the Tarot of Marseille, the Fool card in the first set of arcana features a dog that bites the traveller on the behind as it goes off to meet its destiny. But if we superimpose this onto the the World card in the last arcana – which features a woman we might take to be the Virgin Mary, since she is surrounded by the four apostles – then a new dog appears, whose body is formed by the World's mandorla. It traces out a cosmic circle like the one in Vézelay, but now uniting the beginning and the end of the deck of cards, a circle at whose centre we might now expect to find not only the Virgin Mary but also Mary Magdalene. Did the sculptors, painters, and cartomancers of the Middle Ages want to transmit a message that could not be said out loud, by interspersing their works with clues as to the real nature of Mary Magdalene; and, if so, what were they trying to tell us? We know that, in an esoteric tradition that comes from well before the *Da Vinci Code* she was supposed to be the bride of Christ. But if she may have been God's bitch instead, what does this tell us?

DARWIN'S DOGS

Around the beginning of the nineteenth century, philosophy began to regard the exit from religion as one of its primary aims. One might then expect that it would also want to have done with the dog, and this time for good. But almost the exact opposite is true: the three great atheists of the nineteenth century, Marx, Darwin, and Freud, were all mad about dogs.

Marx obviously didn't agree with Sartre that any anticommunist is a dog, since he had three of them, one named Whiskey, while Engels had a dog called Namenlosen, 'the Nameless'. Freud always had a number of dogs around him, their companionship affording him some relief from the pain caused by his cancer of the jaw – particularly Topsy, the Chow Chow given to him by Marie Bonaparte, who developed the same disease after Freud took her on, as if she were determined to follow her master in whatever he did. As for Darwin, his love for dogs was far beyond the norm. He had five terriers (Nina, Spark, Pincher, Sheila, Polly), a retriever (Bob), a spitz (Snow), a Pointer (Dash) and even a giant Scottish Deerhound (Bran) during his lifetime. It is therefore no coincidence that, thanks to them, some of the mystery of dogs would finally be clarified.

Darwin's *Origin of Species* prompts us to ask whether the domestication of the dog was a mere accident of history, a tumble back down the tree of life, or whether, on the contrary, it was a successful evolutionary strategy. As the biologist Stephen Budiansky quips, the question answers itself: wolves once ruled over all the forests of the world, but there are only a few thousand left today, whereas there are hundreds of millions of dogs ...

We now know that the dog initially evolved in the same way as a parasitical species. Recent canine archaeo-zoological studies, which are based on comparisons between the DNA of dogs and that of wolves, show that the dog appeared in two stages. At first, a new type of wolf detached itself from the primitive species

300,000 years ago, around about the time that *Homo sapiens* appeared. This proto-dog must have been very similar to the wild dogs that still live on the outskirts of numerous cities throughout the world. It approached human habitats in order to eat their waste, like a big rat; at first it was treated accordingly, as vermin. But, because packs of these dogs kept the wolves away from the new human territories, early humans would soon discover in them the qualities that make them our companions today. So that, around 35,000 BC if one is to judge by the first remains of dogs to be found in human tombs, the parasitical relationship gave way to a *symbiotic* one.

The dog developed seductive traits, specifically directed at humans. All signs of wolfish aggression were tempered; the dog no longer rolls back its whisker pads to show its teeth, for example. Its ears became soft, making it the only mammal in its genus to possess this discernible trait, which is associated with the gene for sociability. This new dog literally disguised itself as the happy imbecile with whom we now identify it, because this choice had become its best chance of success. The dog *domesticated us* rather than the other way around, even learning to divine the intention of humans by observing their sclerotics – the whites of their eyes. These white discs, which first appeared in *Australopithecus*, allow one much better than an entirely coloured eye to identify the direction of the gaze when the eye moves. They thus make it possible to anticipate the dangers that arise in the field of vision of a partner some way away – an obvious advantage in the struggle for survival. Apart from humans, the dog is the only animal to have evolved the ability to use this indicator to find out where we are looking (not even monkeys have). Moreover, we know that the dog doesn't use this ability when dealing with other dogs, even though some dogs do have a visible sclererotic – for example the Basset Hound, whose drooping eyelids contribute to its surprisingly human appearance.

Conversely, humans have been able to unburden themselves of a certain number of tasks, particularly those related to attention and vigilance. The human brain has become specialised, as has the dog's, to the point where the cerebral areas of humans and dogs have undergone reciprocal changes; and everything indicates that we have one brain between us, that our brain is never truly complete unless it is paired with a dog's.

In short, humans and dogs have *co-evolved*. Which is to say that, while from the point of the theory of species humans are descended from apes, Darwin might well have considered that they are descended at least as much from dogs. And this is where we come back to our stories of sex and death. For what does this mean if not that the dog is our parent and, in that case, that our mother is the bitch, guardian of the passage that leads from nothingness to human existence?

COMPANION SPECIES
MANIFESTO

In her *Companion Species Manifesto*, the American philosopher Donna Haraway argues that the theory of the co-evolution of humans and dogs obliges us to revisit the division between nature and culture, earth and heaven, master and slave, inherited from Platonism and monotheism. As she writes, monotheism would have us believe that there are preexisting and fixed identities – man and animal, God and his creatures – and that, *in addition*, a link must then be created between the two, a link that therefore necessarily becomes a detestable bond of subordination. Within this framework, the dog, whose destiny is to belong to both kingdoms, is necessarily consigned to a kind of unthinkable status, condemned to ontological homelessness. And the same is true of humans within the context of religion: always too earthbound for heaven yet too celestial for the earth, humans can never find their rightful place between earth and heaven. Humans will always hate nature, though they will hate culture just as much. They will forever hate themselves.

Haraway thinks differently. In her view, the dog invites us to think of ourselves as composite, *prosthetic* beings, forming one sole being with two faces, one single entity divided between domesticated nature and culture made wild. In what is ultimately a rather pagan approach, she sings the praises of a new, impure body in which cyborg and animal, parasite and host cannot be disentangled from each other and that is specifically created through the practice of training, which she unexpectedly praises.

As Haraway observes, training is unbearable for us because it reminds us of our own narcissistic wounds (and also, it is true, because in the past it was carried out in barbaric ways). And yet there is something entirely different at stake here. You don't train a dog by yelling at it or beating it, but by rewarding, encouraging, and praising it – and above all by observing it. For training begins with the dog, not with the human. A dog sits down spontaneously: you reward this behaviour in order to create, in the dog, a pleasant association between the seated position and the word 'sit'. It is only by force of repetition that the dog ends up confusing consequence (the word 'sit') with cause (sitting down). In other words, to train an animal is to attain a troubling insight into the way in which nature itself functions: bottom-up, not top-down. To train a dog is to become dog oneself, rather than to make the dog into one of us.

So what if we do erase the division between culture and nature, as Haraway invites us to? Does this mean that we're done with it? Monotheism, too, wished to abolish the separation between earth and heaven; and monotheism, too, was merely a matter of training. Couldn't it be that, as far as this relationship between opposites is concerned, paganism and monotheism are, strictly, the same thing in different forms? Obviously, Haraway is right to say that human and animal do not preexist each other, that they do not constitute distinct essences any more than human and God do. After all, the human is an animal like any other. But in that case, in order for the human to separate itself from the animals, the animal had to separate *from itself*. It had to split into two. Shouldn't we then say, more faithfully to Darwin's thinking, that what is really decisive about the dog, its real mystery, is not that it co-evolved with humans, but that it broke evolution itself in two? That dogs *invented what escapes, transcends, and opposes itself to the animal kingdom?*

Ecce canis

Biologists have a very vivid way of explaining an enigma different from that of the birth of the human: the birth of life itself.

Imagine a pool table full of balls rolling in all directions – a representation of the primordial chaos in which atoms are continually colliding. Now place a pool cue across the table. The balls continue to collide, but whenever they touch the cue, it acts like a perfect shock absorber. The disorderly energy of each ball is absorbed and transmitted by the cue in the form of a continuous energy, proportionate to the sum of the energies of all the balls. As difficult as it might be to imagine how the cue could extract this energy and use it, by means of some sort of telescopic arm, for example, suppose that it could start moving and reorganising the balls on one side of the table, directing one here, one there, or even stealing 'wild' balls from one side in order to increase its personal stock of 'domestic' balls on the other. In this way an organised system would emerge from the chaos: a homeostatic whole made possible through the capture of the disordered energy of the pool balls and through its conversion it into usable energy with the help of the cue that divides the table.

The conclusion biologists draw from this rudimentary thought experiment is that life must be born from a *membrane*: it's a link that cuts off or filters one part from another and thereby allows a chaotic system to become ordered. If we are to suppose that culture emerged from nature the same way life emerged from chaos, it must have done so by means of a membrane of the same kind.

On the basis of this thought experiment we might put forward the following hypothesis: the dog was this membrane. It was like a skin for humans, a second skin, or rather a *first* skin – the external limit that allowed the birth of the interiority that makes humans human.

This might be the ultimate meaning of the dog's fidelity. It is not a derivative kind of faith. It is a faith more primordial than monotheism, a faith without psychology, without God, and even without humans: a *molecular fidelity*. Fidelity is that which forges a bond. As such, it is that which permits things to hold together. Fidelity traces a line, stretches out a thread – it outlines a membrane, just as the electromagnetic relations between atoms ensure the rigidity of the pool cue. The fidelity of dogs is what gives them their essential capability to stick together, to form a barrier against the world, to absorb the savagery of nature and *to transmit it back in the form of affection.*

In a broad sense, the dog is the animal that links and holds together all that is, starting with its fellow creatures. And indeed it is an extraordinary and always a joyful thing to see how indifferent dogs are to one another's race, size, and age and how they enjoy forming little bands instantaneously. Dogs are not visual creatures. They know nothing of distance – or of decency, which is another name for distance. They are olfactory creatures. They need to smell, to touch, to rub up against things. They need to stick together like magnets. Dogs are nature's communists. With all due respect to those who like to depict them as police, in the style of Rin Tin Tin, fond of order and of the baton, dogs are rather lefties like Kanellos, the dog of the Greek revolts of the summer of 2007, like Petardo, the dog of the Bolivian protestors, and like the dog in Gustave Courbet's *A Burial at Ornans*, who looks on as the Paris Commune is buried. It's not that they love their masters – they love togetherness. Ethnologists have recently discovered that, when feral dogs are together, they *sneeze* to vote on decisions as a group. Not barking, but sneezing: that's the secret tongue of dogs, maybe the true, democratic, origin of spoken language even.

DOG YEARS

Freud writes that the reasons why 'one can love an animal like Topsy (or Jofi) with such extraordinary intensity' are related to its 'affection without ambivalence, the simplicity of life free from the almost unbearable conflicts of civilisation, the beauty of an existence complete in itself' (letter to Marie Bonaparte).

We would be hard put to say it any better than this: what the dog transmits to humans is a livable world, a world stripped of all its imperfections, cushioned from all of its blows. Except that, contra Freud, it is not primarily the conflicts of 'civilisation' that the dog keeps at bay, but the conflicts of nature itself.

Hunters distinguish between four types of dog: retrievers, scent hounds, Bloodhounds, and Pointers. Their tasks are respectively to bring back dead game, to pursue the quarry, to track down wounded prey, and to locate a living animal for the hunter. In the last case, the dog must draw near to the animal and then freeze until its master arrives. Then it must creep toward the animal to get as close as possible and point it out. All that remains is for the hunter to aim and fire. Of the four types of hunting dogs, the Pointer is perhaps the one that goes most strongly against its own nature in carrying out its allotted task. But at the same time it is in *pointing* that it comes closest to fulfilling itself.

The dog is a 'dark precursor', that negative trace that precedes the appearance of lightning in the sky. Like Goya's painted dog, only its head emerging from the dividing line between a black wall and a heap of yellow sand, it exists not so much in the moment when day turns to night as in the moment when day *fractures* night. Dogs are vertical beings: they plunge into the subsoil from which the odours of blood and decay rise to their nostrils, and they communicate with the moon, serenading it with their nocturnal howls.

As the ancients sensed, dogs do indeed have a certain relation to time – but not so much to its passage as to its intensity. Dogs are masters of time, particularly when they see with their snouts rather than with their eyes. For an odour persists through time. To pick up a scent is to know that an animal *has passed through*. To smell a pregnant female is to know that she *will give birth*. In short, to smell is always to live in the past or in the future, so that it is dogs that, in the most ancient times, relieved us from being always *present* in the world, always on the lookout. And in doing so it was they who opened up *free time* for us – something without which no culture, no humanity would have been possible. As with the perfectly still Welsh Guards of the English Crown in their tall bearskin hats, we might say of dogs that all of their energy goes into literally *killing time*. And, who knows, perhaps this is why they live such short lives. Dogs die so that we may live, just as the Baptist had to decrease in order for Christ to increase, and just as Anubis himself had to step back to make way for John.

In a secret corner of Hyde Park there is a hidden dog cemetery, arranged just like a human cemetery, with marble tombs and family vaults upon which are graven doggy names that, in this context, one cannot help but find vaguely obscene, embarrassing in their involuntary tackiness: Rocky, Frisk, Dolly. But if we consider these headstones as so many plaques dedicated to unknown soldiers, of whom all that remained was a surname on a medal or embroidered inside a jacket collar, then they take on an entirely different aspect. All dogs may be considered combatants who died for humanity. They are all like those 'animals in war' to whom monuments are sometimes erected. Rocky, Frisk, and Dolly, small dogs with ridiculous names, wheezy little rascals, cute sausages with goofy smiles, be comforted: as Luther assured his dog Tölpel, *thou too in Resurrection shall have a little golden tail.*

PORTRAIT OF THE PHILOSOPHER AS A DOG

Some masters, all too aware of the frightening speed at which dogs pass away, replace them as they approach the end of their lives, often with a dog of the same breed. Sometimes they even give the successor the same name (as in the case of Yves Saint Laurent's Bulldog, of which there have been four generations, almost four 'models': Moujik, Moujik II, Moujik III, and Moujik IV). In this way they are accompanied throughout their entire lives by a sort of unique dog, a generic dog whose unchanged form receives multiple transmigrated souls. Although it may seem barbarous, and even though I personally cannot bring myself to do it, it seems to me that this is an appropriate way to respect the dog's particular relation to time.

Many grieving dog owners feel as if they have lost a child, but in my own experience it has felt more like being *orphaned*, as if it were not a child I had lost, but a parent. It is difficult to think of any way to describe the pain of someone who has lost a child, there is no word for it in English. But there is another cause for feeling that one is the 'orphan' of a dog: it's that the dog is perhaps just as much a father or mother as it is a child, and one would be more correct to call it affectionately 'dada' or 'mama' than 'little darling' or 'baby'.

In *Thy Servant a Dog*, Kipling has Boots and Slippers, his little Scottish Terriers, say that they 'help' the master to smoke his pipe or to read his newspaper. Along the same lines, I like to think that the dog is the animal that 'helps' us to be, throughout our entire lives. The dog is a mother to us. Another myth, one that would have grabbed Freud's attention, tells us as much: the myth of the wolf child, the orphan raised by a female dog.

We all know the story of the founding of Rome, the city that claimed to be the cradle of *humanitas*. It involves two twins, just like Xolotl and the Koma-Inu: Romulus and Remus, children of the god Mars and of a vestal, Rhea Silvia. Snatched by Silvia's brother and cast adrift on a river, these twins are retrieved at the foot of the Palatine Hill by a she-wolf, who raises them until they are old enough to avenge themselves of their uncle and found a city. The story is more complicated, however, since the Latin noun for 'she-wolf', *lupa*, also means 'prostitute'. But is this so surprising? We have seen this analogy between dog and woman crop up again and again. And now perhaps we begin to understand its meaning: it concerns in particular the pregnant woman, who resembles a dog insofar as she is also a membrane, a placenta. She is guardian of the frontier that runs between excess and void, from which all life proceeds. In Greek, *kuōn*, 'dog', and *kuō*, 'to be pregnant', 'to conceive', are very closely related words; by extension, 'conceive' in the sense of 'think' can also mean 'have puppies'. The dog, or rather the bitch, the pregnant woman, and philosophy are seemingly one and the same.

We know of at least one philosopher who understood the bond between philosopher and dog: Diogenes, who, by making himself a Cynic (*Kuōn*, *Kunikos*), portrayed himself as a woman 'pregnant' with ideas. According to some, Jesus was a late disciple of the school of Diogenes. One would explain the other. But nothing speaks more clearly of this knotting together of humanity and the dog under the sign of sexuality and philosophy than another Greek character, albeit a legendary one this time: Oedipus.

OEDIPUS REX

Oedipus' myth revolves around a fantastic creature known as the Sphinx. She happens to be a bitch, even though she is often mistaken for a lion. The Sphinx is the daughter of Orthos (the twin brother of Cerberus), and dogs don't make cats. Now, it is already remarkable that in ancient Greek her name – which originally designated a kind of ape and was applied metaphorically to 'rapacious' persons – derives from the verb *sphingō* (σφίγγω), 'bind tight', and belongs in the same family as *sphinktēr* (σφιγκτήρ), which was used to designate anything that binds tight, knots, and locks – 'lace', 'band', '(draw)string' – and also the muscle that opens and closes an aperture ('sphincter' is a nice loan word from ancient Greek into the English language). It is yet more extraordinary that the one who manages to undo the Sphinx, king to be Oedipus, appears himself to be a dog (named Rex).

How can we tell? Rare vase fragments dating from the sixth century show Oedipus in the form of a dog. And one little detail really gives it away: his name. Oedipus means 'swollen foot' (the name is a compound of *oideō* 'I swell', as in 'oedema', and *pous*, *podos* 'foot'). This name reflects the fact that the shepherd who had brought Oedipus to be killed on Mount Cithaeron pierced his ankle so as to thread a cord through it, in order to carry him on his shoulder. But that doesn't make any sense. We find no example of carrying anyone in that manner in ancient literature. Yet *dogs* were indeed tied up like this: a cord was passed through the tarsus (the point where the tibia starts and can be easily pierced, between the bone and the tendon), in order to make sure that they did not pull on their chain. So Oedipus might have rather been tied to a stick on top of Mount Cithaeron and left to die that way, like a dog. Maybe this is why it is also said that Diogenes the Cynic, Diogenes the man dog, died of an 'injury to the foot'.

Oedipus is the dog with a swollen foot. This matters because his feet play an important role in the dénouement of his encounter with the Sphinx. For the riddle that she poses to him turns above all on resolving the mystery of 'standing upright': 'Who walks on four feet in the morning, two at midday, and three in the evening?' If Oedipus manages to answer 'man', this is because he has 'knowledge of feet' (a play on words constructed on the homophony between *oideō*, which means 'I swell', and *oida*, which means 'I know'). In other words, Oedipus is a dog that *knows how to stand on two feet*. In return, the Sphinx, mistress of knots (in the literal and figurative senses – one's brain gets 'tied in knots' when trying to solve her riddles), undoes the 'drawstring' that binds him. By doing so, she frees the man who was in the dog.

In reality the myth of Oedipus is not primarily about the prohibition of incest or parricide, as Freud says; it is a myth about the mystery of hominisation, the enigma of the humans' separation from animals, their being the only species capable of standing upright, along with bears, apes and dogs, albeit briefly. Incest and parricide only appear insofar as they are related to this question. In fact, one might wonder whence Oedipus gets his knowledge of feet. And this is where sexuality comes into the picture. If the dog pierces the riddle and penetrates the lock of the prophetess with his swollen foot, it is obvious that he is *erect* and that it is not just his front legs that have risen up, but also his penis. Oedipus owes his knowledge of feet not to his intelligence but to his body, to his *desire*, to the fact that he is traversed by a strange desire that makes him rise up.

Of course, all mammals have erections, and Oedipus's is therefore not enough to demarcate human from animal, except that Oedipus has a pierced foot, a mutilated sex – an extra fact that says something particular about *human* erections: unlike other animals, human males have no bone inside their penis. The absence of this bone, called the *baculum*, the 'little stick', did not pass unnoticed by our ancestors. According to certain exegetes, this bone is Adam's rib, from which Eve was made. In the riddle of the Sphinx, it is the cane that helps humans to walk when they reach old age.

So Oedipus is not an animal like any other. It is because he can get wood without a *baculum* that he can stand upright. This is the deepest meaning of his encounter with the bitch philosopher. The Oedipus myth says that there is a link between the upright posture that is the foundation of hominisation and the absence of this bone, and more particularly that a dog holds the secret of the absence of this bone, that a dog that lost his bone is the bridge between animal and man.

Hence there remains this one question: Why does Oedipus no longer have it? What is it that now holds up the *erection* of the aptly named *Homo erectus*, if it is no longer a stick or a cane? We know that this absence is linked to the mutilation inflicted on him after his mother gave him to a shepherd to take away from her, having learned from the Pythia that he would be an incestuous parricide. We also know that he has just killed his father in error, at a crossroads, fulfilling the first act of the prophecy. The crime is thus linked to the process of hominisation – or rather hominisation is some sort of crime, but in what sense? Only another myth involving dogs, humans, eroticism and murder gives away the answer: now we need to talk about the oldest, most secret of all myths of ancient Greece.

Sons of a Bitch

In the Greek town of Eleusis, once a year, Demeter, goddess of the earth, was celebrated and thanked for having given mankind the gift of agriculture. The story is that after Hades, god of the underworld, stole away Demeter's daughter Persephone, Demeter threatened to stop the wheat from growing if he wouldn't return her, so that Zeus had to promise that Persephone would be allowed to spend six months of the year (spring and summer) with her mother, the other six months (autumn and winter) with her husband. It was during harvest time, at the beginning of September, that the hierophants initiated a select few into the secrets of the seasonal cycle, the mysteries of death and renewal. Principal among the instruments of this initiation was the 'potion' (*kukeōn*, κυκεών). This beverage, similar to wine, possibly mixed with fermented wheat or hallucinogenic rye spurs, brought on visions and trances that were like a visit to the spirit realm. It represented the first drink Demeter brought to her lips after having almost let herself die of hunger because of her sorrow. A long preparation was required, however, before the *kukeōn* could be drunk. This preparation included obscene rites that consisted in manipulating statuettes in the form of dildos and eating cakes in the form of vulvas. These were meant to recall what happened just after Demeter regained her strength: her encounter with a woman going by the name of Baubo, in whose house she was living, and who restored the goddess's appetite, and indeed her *joy*, by lifting her robe and showing Demeter her vulva.

What was it that so delighted Demeter about seeing Baubo's genitals? No one really knows, but there are multiple examples in numerous cultures of similar acts of exhibitionism that give us an idea. In this particular case, statuettes of Baubo have even been found. They represent a woman lifting her skirts and showing her stomach, upon which a face is drawn: her breasts are its eyes, her navel its mouth, and her pubic area its bearded chin. We also know that the common noun *baubō* ('womb', 'stomach') could be associated with words that meant '[lull to] sleep' (*baubaō*) and, by extension, to be a nurse or a nanny (*baukalaō*; so Baubo would be she who puts you to beddy-byes); also 'dildo' (so Baubo is a sort of *baculum*); and finally 'bark' (*baüzō*, 'cry bau bau' – still the way in which most Latin languages transcribe a dog's bark, as in our 'bow wow'). In other words, Demeter's return to life – and, with hers, that of the whole of nature – could be linked to some kind of canine intervention.

This first intrusion of a dog into the Eleusinian mysteries is no isolated case. In fact there are so many others that, when Hercules has to fulfil his twelfth task – to steal Cerberus, the hound of Hades – he first goes to be initiated at Eleusis. The couple made up of Persephone and Demeter is very similar to that formed by the goddess Isis, the great bitch dog of Egypt, and Anubis, midway between the kingdom of the dead and that of the living, between cultivated nature and wild nature. They, too, have dog servants, foremost among them Hecate, an infernal divinity associated with the moon who is represented in the form of a bitch. And, finally, they are sometimes confused with Artemis, goddess of hunting, and her pack of dogs. Indeed, sometimes Persephone, Artemis, and Hecate are condensed into a single divinity with three heads, one of which is a dog's head. As for Baubo herself, she resembles Anubis's daughter, Kebehout, who helped her. The *kukeōn* she offers to Demeter to bring her back to life (and, with her, all of nature) is reminiscent of the Sa drunk by the worshippers of Isis (the Vedic soma, a ritual drink). And if she also barks, as is said, we might suppose her to be a dog with an *open mouth*.

Now, looking into the mouth of a dog was one of two major taboos of ancient Egyptian culture, the other one being *menstruation*. A first corner of the veil is lifted on the mystery of Baubo's exhibitionism: if she has her mouth open, it hints at the fact that *she has her period*, and the head of a bearded man that she unveils before Demeter is thus a *severed head*, with blood flowing out from under the beard, that is to say the pubis. This explains why Demeter laughs: it is because Baubo, showing her the bloody head of her daughter's rapist, essentially says to her: 'We'll cut off their heads, all those bastards', or even: 'We'll cut off their dicks' – a dick that Baubo also is, since she is a dildo or *baculum* (*baubō*).

Upon this, Demeter regains her appetite and drinks the red liquid that her servant offers her. How better to say that she drinks the blood of anger, which is at once the blood of Baubo's period and the metaphor of the blood gushing from the castrated penis of the god who took away her loved one? Demeter, whose threat of agricultural *sterility* denotes the fact that her periods have stopped because of anorexia, drinks the *kukeōn* after having seen Baubo's belly, as if to signify that she is menstruating again, that she is once more fertile and that there is therefore a link between nature, once more *standing up*, periods, and the blood of castration. This is a link we are all aware of – namely that a woman can only bear children between the time when she first begins to menstruate and the time she ceases to menstruate; but it must have been extraordinarily mysterious to our ancestors, since it linked fertility to a wound and to death.

Our ancient mystery game is almost complete. We have a severed head that probably stands for a severed penis, or at least a severed dildo, a wooden penis, Oedipus's missing *baculum*, whence he gets his swollen foot and his knowledge of bipedality. We have a red potion that stand for periods and the blood of the wounded penis, and the strange sight of Demeter somehow drinking both. And we have dogs, or rather bitches: a mother looking for her stolen one. And all of this relates to the question set by the Winged Bitch (the Sphinx): How did the first man stand up? And why did he have to kill his father and make love to his mother in order to do it?

I suggest the following story. What all this tells us in coded language – because it is highly indecent, and ancient Greeks were very modest – is that once upon a time there lived a god, the mightiest of all, the god of death, Hades, the hunter, also known as Orion, *father* of all living beings; he ravished *mother* nature and stole her away into his lair. She, at the time, lived in the form of a bitch, walking on all fours, the daughter of the great cosmic bitch (Canis Minor, aka Persephone, daughter of Canis Major, Demeter). While he attempted to rape her, she turned on him and bit a piece off his penis, tearing off his *baculum*. That stick, along with all its blood, she swallowed and drank; thus it made her rigid like a stick or, more exactly, permitted the boy child born of that monstrous union, half god half dog, to *stand up* on his two feet after drinking the blood of his father in her womb – in other words, to get hard without a stick.

This newborn is *man*, the human male himself, literally the son of a bitch. In Egypt he was called Horus, son of Isis and Osiris, and was precisely the first pharaoh, the founder of human civilisation. In ancient Greece he was Dionysus the *twice born*, protector of nature and giver of wine, a bridge between savagery and culture. In the Oedipus myth he is the *upright dog* that stands up to the Sphinx after having bitten his own father to death, before making love to his own mother. In everyday life, he is any man.

BLOODHOUNDS

'Eleusis' derives from the Greek *eleusis* (ἔλευσις), 'coming', 'arrival' – by extension, into the world. That is to say that the Eleusinian mysteries celebrated the *hierogamy* (sacred marriage) between the great primordial she-dog and the god of death who presided over the coming into the world of the human species – they were the fundamental explanation of the mystery of the birth of civilisation, and perhaps the most ancient, albeit the most silenced, the most difficult to speak of all myths, for the most authentically scandalous.

Still, some celebrate it openly, even today, and have done so for all eternity: the Inuits – those who owe their name to the word *inu*, 'dog' (which is found in Japanese, and one whose bearers is perhaps the ancestor of Inpu/

Anubis). They are faithful to the religion according to which they were born of the great bitch Inu and are therefore the 'dog people' or 'dog men'. Inu and the god of chaos came together to give birth to humanity, they say, just like Hades and Persephone, or like Isis and Osiris – that is to say, like Sirius and Orion: Canis Major and the constellation of the Hunter. But others have traditionally kept quiet about it. Indeed, at Eleusis in particular, the most taboo things were practised: menstrual blood was probably drunk to celebrate this birth, in memory of the blood that had flowed from the god's penis; this turned the cursed periods into a productive transgression and, by analogy, made it possible to cross the frontier that separates the kingdom of the living from that of the dead, as psychopomp dogs did.

We cannot rule out the possibility that the water that *changes into wine*, which Christians still drink today in order to be reborn in Christ, is an echo of this same fundamental myth. Easter, the festival of resurrection, of spring, and of the moon (represented by Easter *eggs*) would on this account be a remarkable reworking of the Eleusinian mysteries, accompanied by its two emblems: Lepus, the thaumaturgical Easter 'bunny' who comes back each winter, as if *resuscitated* – like Dionysus and Horus; and Columba, the dove of the holy ghost whose 'wings' are none other than what replaces the *baculum* after it has been eaten, the new way man has to stand upright without a stick. The dove is a winged dog, like the Sphinx – or, better, a winged phallus, like those amulets the Romans loved to carry with them for luck and that have a bell attached to the end of the glans, as on a dog's collar. As for Mary Magdalene, the reason why she continued to be celebrated in silence becomes evident: a vestigial figure of the canine myths of antiquity, she would not be the bride of Christ but the Virgin Mary's double: one the mother of Christ, the other the mother of all humanity.

During the Middle Ages, the Lancelot–Grail cycle brought the memory of this strange story to life in the collective unconscious. The quest for a cup of blood that would make one immortal is a clear sign of this, and the idea that it had perhaps been brought from the Orient by Mary Magdalene, as some legends suggest, only goes to confirm it. In this new folklore there emerged above all the legend of the werewolf and of the terrifying magical 'black dog', Barghest – a dog of whom it is said that anyone crossing its path would soon die, and whose name could mean literally the 'spirit of the tomb' (it might be a compound of the German *Geist*, 'spirit', and the English funeral 'bier' or pyre).

Eighteenth-century German mystic Nikolaus von Zinzendorf's theology of 'blood and wounds' was also linked to the memory of these legends. Combining Luther's love of dogs with the highly protestant cult of the *physical* death of God, one of his canticles states that he who, *like a poor little dog*, licks the bloody wounds of Jesus Christ, possesses true simplicity – and of course here we recognise Balak, the dog who licks the blood of Israel (e.g. 1 Kings 21:19, 22:38). The Viennese actionist Hermann Nitsch, who was fond of bloody ceremonies, may well have been remembering this, as did Joseph Beuys, holding in his arms a dead hare (*lepus*), its face covered in gold like a Renaissance Pietà, and taunting a caged coyote with a 'cane', also a *baculum*. Before them, Friedrich Nietzsche, signing his final letters 'Dionysos, or the Crucified', would also have known all about Easter and Eleusis.

Finally, two other much celebrated pop culture characters present their own version of this profound mystery, quite obviously for anyone who knows what to look for: Little Red Riding Hood and Count Dracula. Little Red Riding Hood, who is most certainly a little boy rather than a girl (up to the nineteenth century, red was a colour for boys, blue for girls) is devoured – castrated, then – during a sexual act that goes against nature, with his grandmother, who turns out in fact to be a wolf, or more exactly a dog, if we consider that a dog is precisely a *wolf in grandma's clothing*. As for Dracula, he appears at the beginning of Bram Stoker's novel in the form of a 'black dog', Barghest, leaping from the bridge of a sinking Russian ship off the English coast near Whitby – a ship named *Demeter*. Like the black dog, he will appear again later at nightfall – that is, with the moon, the star of Hecate, because the lunar cycle is also the menstrual cycle, which is truly the source of the blood he drinks and the reason why it procures him immortality, as once did the *kukeōn* and the soma. Like the dog, he bites – but, even better, he infects those whom he bites. Anyone who is bitten becomes a vampire too, in the same way one might become rabid when bitten – and in antiquity rabies was believed to be treatable precisely by spreading menstrual blood on the bite, according to the age-old principle of healing evil with evil. In the same spirit, at the Roman festival of

Canicula, red dogs were sacrificed to calm the solar star, the rabid star, because it was believed that redheads were the fruit of making love during menstruation.

Dracula, and the wolf disguised as a grandmother, and the Hound of the Baskervilles in Arthur Conan Doyle's eponymous novel, along with the devil who appears in the form of a black beard at the end of Goethe's *Faust*: each in its own way incarnates the fundamental ambiguity of the canine, as understood since ancient Egypt – and particularly its sexual ambiguity. But here the dog is not just the *go-between* of life and death, nature and culture, masculine and feminine, it is also the *creator* of culture, the creator of humanity. It is not the domesticated but the domesticator; it is the great civiliser, and this is so, paradoxically, because it is the *great castrator*.

The celebrated Egyptian Tale of Two Brothers tells of how the bull Bata castrated himself out of shame, after the wife of the dog Anubis attempted to seduce him. This tale presents the final example, or the originary matrix, of the whole story: for Bata (Aldebaran) did not cut his penis off; it was bitten off by Anubis, who thereby transformed the bull into a cow, civilising it and simultaneously founding civilisation, just as Romulus and Remus founded Rome after having suckled at the teat of the Capitoline bitch, drinking, with her milk, the blood of the divine father.

A TERGO, MORE FERARUM

'All that I care for is dogs, that and nothing else. For what is there actually except our own species? To whom else can one appeal in the wide and empty world? All knowledge, the totality of all questions and all answers, is contained in the dog.' Thus speaks another dog, in a novella by Franz Kafka of which only a fragment remains, 'Investigations of a Dog'.

It is easy to see this 'dog philosopher' as another manifestation of Kafka's usual irony about claims to wisdom, from whatever quarter they may come. But Kafka sincerely loved dogs, as we can tell from the most famous photograph of the writer, where he is seen affectionately holding by the ear a German Shepherd who poses between him and his sweetheart, Julie

Szokoll. Another reading of this work could therefore be that it is a more personal and sincere representation of Kafka himself as a dog – a hungry, stray, beaten-down dog: a representation of the condition of the Jews of early twentieth-century racist Mitteleuropa. But, in that case, what is this very particular 'knowledge' of dogs he speaks of here?

The rest of the story does not say. Or rather, as our canine narrator adds soon afterward, *dogs themselves refuse to reveal it*. The dog is 'more secretive of his knowledge than of the places where good food can be found'. Even he, the narrator, a dog, cannot reveal what he knows. As is often the case in Kafka, the truth withdraws at the very point where it ought to reveal itself.

Dogs 'lack only speech', it seems. But are we so sure of that? Can we be so sure that they don't just keep quiet out of fear of being punished for the secrets, great and small, that they know about us? Or is it perhaps that they have lost their tongue, like a person struck dumb with fear ... or with mad laughter, like Demeter? Or is it that they are like the hierophants of Eleusis, bound together by the secrets they keep, by the obligation to say nothing of what happened during the initiation rite during which they spoke of matters as taboo as they were sacred?

Kafka suggests as much when he, in turn, makes the dog into a representation of Oedipus. His narrator is crushed by guilt, but cannot understand its source. What is more, we learn that he has walked on 'four paws' since he was young; that during his adolescence he encounters strange 'dog musicians' who walked on 'two paws', and in his old age a hunting dog who 'trails his left hind leg behind him' (and who therefore walks on 'three paws') … How could Kafka have made it any plainer that he understood that the dog knows *what* the human being is and that, if he does not tell, it is out of sheer decency? For ultimately the human is nothing but a 'stand-up dog' – that is to say, a boner.

This is also what is revealed by Deleuze's cruel phrase about the dog as the 'shame of the animal kingdom', if only in the form of a *lapsus linguae*, slip of tongue. Even in this rare moment of beastly stupidity Deleuze still displays a touch of genius, for in saying this he puts his finger on an essential point: that the dog is in some way linked to shame. Only it is *our* shame that dogs carry with them, our pudenda. And unconsciously we realise this when we *castrate* them, parade them through the streets offering them up to the caress of all comers, like proud exhibitionists – and get them excited with bits of wood, with *Baubo's baculum*.

Dogs know our shame: this is their secret and the reason why they say nothing. And it is also, no doubt, why sometimes we can blame them – blame them for knowing so much about us. This is why we prefer to hide them away. It's the reason why dogs appear so little in our culture – or only as a travesty, in the form of a lion or a bear, symbols of an aspirational, imperial, properly masculine phallus, celebrated in the form of denial, whereas in reality dogs are everywhere, the dog is *in us*, the dog *is* us. If the dog is nowhere to be seen, if it is forgotten, ridiculed, or, on the contrary, becomes a subject of adulation to the point of obsession, the most profound reason for this is to be found here: that the dog is nothing but the impossible name of our origin, the image that no one can bear to see, the image of the coitus that birthed us.

This is the ultimate meaning of the 'repression' Freud discovered when he worked out the meaning of the

Oedipus complex in psychoanalysing 'the wolf man', who found that he was in fact a 'dog man' – since, as Freud remarks, the dog is never anything but a 'castrated wolf'. Every child who accidentally discovers his parents having sex *a tergo, more ferarum*, 'from behind like animals', will inevitably identify his mother with a 'big dog' and will consequently see himself as a little dog, while trying to forget what he saw and couldn't understand except as some form of violence. And yet, in doing so, all he will manage to do is bury the dog that he saw *in himself*, just as Oedipus ended up putting out his own eyes.

The unconscious is a black dog. It is that 'tomb of the spirit' in which lurk the barghests, all the werewolves, the *wolves in us*, which haunt us on nights when the moon is full.

THE MARK OF CAIN

I have placed this book under the sign of joy and wisdom, the great joy of the dog; and the riddle, the scandal underpinning this joy. The answer to this riddle is the very same answer that Oedipus gave to the Sphinx, the drink that Baubo gave to Demeter, and the Grand Guignol-style story that Freud and Darwin presented to humanity about its origins and that made it scream. The dog is joyous because it made man, because it *erected* the human male *like a sex*, and it did so by biting the genitals of the God of the underworld, just as a dog bites the Fool in the tarot. The dog laughs like Demeter at the great joke he has made of death.

The dog allowed the human to give birth to itself. As we have seen, the dog made its body into a membrane so as to keep the external world at bay. But it also allowed humans to give birth to themselves *psychically*. God and devil, protector and destroyer, just like the ambiguous mother who is also good and bad, feeder and frustrator, 'talking' vagina and 'toothed' vagina, the dog made a membrane of its body *inside* our world. The dog sheltered our unconscious within it, in the space outlined by the limits of repression, and, along with the unconscious, desire, the *tension* of the membrane, whence sprang the desire that keeps us upright, the 'wings' of desire that now replace our stick. So it is that the invention of the human really took place by way of a round trip between human and dog in which one cannot be distinguished from the other.

Dog created the human so that the human could win the war of evolution in his place. The dog invented culture so that nature could transcend itself and protect it in return. The date of the transition from proto-dog to domesticated dog testifies to this: this transition occurs in the same era during which *Homo sapiens* produced the first cave paintings – in other words, at the moment when humans *birthed* themselves, when they entered properly into culture and into history.

Reciprocally, humans invented themselves thanks to the dog. It is in the dog's image that they entered into the world of desire, undoing the natural regime of need and acceding to the kingdom of culture. It is by making themselves dogs that they were *re-born* in a new body, but one that will never decay: a spiritual body, that of the 'self-consciousness' that is the foundation of properly human dignity.

The human descends from the dog, and so the joy of the dog is very much like the joy of parents happy to have transmitted their genes to their descendants. The dog has created a demi-god; so, if he acts so cool, it's because he has done his job. He no longer has anything to do. He is on holiday for the rest of his life, a perpetual flâneur, a tourist of existence. Not a handsome hobo like the hero of *The Lady and the Tramp*, not even a 'celestial' one, but a retired ambassador, a marshal of the empire returned from his many wars; he is the true king of the animals. Puppies walk with their shoulders straight, pulling on their leash like young officers in a hurry to get on; old dogs make haste slowly, like cardinals who have seen it all. With their long aristocratic pedigree names, their regimental surnames, together they form the Company of Dogs, just as there is a Company of Jesus.

But dogs are still more joyous than that, with a joy that is more tender, almost bawdy, because the human they have invented holds no secrets for them. Just as Demeter laughs when she sees the severed head beneath Baubo's skirts, the dog is joyful because this human male whom he can now admire, this big man he has made, the dog knows who he is, he has seen his sex, and he has seen him as a sex. He has seen him as a mother sees her child. And this is why the dog plays so happily with his masters: because he is not afraid of being ridiculous in front of them – they who are so much more ridiculous than he could ever be. Sure enough, the word 'imbecile' comes from 'lacking a *baculum*' in Latin (*imbecillus*, 'weak'). It does not apply do dogs so much as it does to us.

After Cain had committed his crime, it is written in Genesis that God gave him a 'mark' to protect him from men who would punish him. On the nature of this mark, however, nothing is said, so that the 'mark of Cain' has excited the imagination of many exegetes. Since it would have had to be something repugnant, some have believed that it referred to leprosy: Cain could not be touched by others while he continued to atone for Abel. Others have suggested that it was more defensive, like a bull's horn pushing through his forehead. But one Midrash suggests that God gave a dog to Cain, and that this dog was his mark. We could make sense of this idea by considering that the dog was 'impure', and therefore could have protected Cain from vengeance while also being a sign of infamy. But another explanation is more probable. For, each time the dog appears in the Midrash, it is used as a metaphor for sex. The dog designates the uncircumcised, those who have an obscene penis. So we might imagine that what the author of the Midrash was trying to say by suggesting that the mark of Cain was a dog is that the mark of Cain was an enormous penis, so large that it would have been at once an object of fascination and one of repulsion, a monster, a fairground freak. This is all the more plausible given the link between dog and phallus, along with the fact that, throughout antiquity, to have a small penis was a mark of civilisation, as we can see in Greek and Roman statuary.

Ever since this happened, we males have carried between our legs not a sex but a dog, which stands up on its two legs, in a ridiculous manner, whenever it feels like it and never for very long, like a poodle, or the musician dogs in Kafka's story. Such is the reciprocal outcome of this story – at which we can only laugh, along with the dogs themselves.

THE BIG BARK

A few years ago now, the artist Pierre Huyghe sent a dog walking down the aisles of the Centre Pompidou. It was a Podenco, the primitive dog breed to which Anubis, Xolotl, and the Sphinx probably belonged; but, unlike the Egyptian and Aztec gods, this was an entirely white one, with a bright purple paw. Marked by this strange sign of civilisation, she looked like a dog that had made the return trip from death back to life. But what was perhaps more troubling was that this dog was called Human. She forced the visitor to ask which of the two was the animal.

Is it the case that, when the Sphinx's question 'Who am I?' is posed to a human, the response must be, bizarrely, 'I am a dog' – but, inversely, when it is posed to a dog the response must be 'I am a human'? Alberto Giacometti gave a similar answer to Jean Genet when asked why he, who only sculpted *Walking Men I*, had made a sculpture of a dog: 'It's me. One day I saw myself in the street like that. I was the dog.' And as for Man Ray, William Wegman's aptly named Weimaraner, when he contemplates his portrait he seems to say: '*I'm the Man, Ray.*'

Ancient dogs such as the Komainu do not go two by two only to express the duality of the world. They are twofold so as to remind us that human and dog were conceived as mirror each other, or more exactly that the human appears in the implied empty place *between* two dogs, between the imaginary dog and the real dog, who are thus referred back to their image and to their barkings, 'a' and 'um' – to infinity.

When the snow lion of Siddhartha roars, he makes heard the 'great void' (*śūnyatā*) that marks the moment of karmic awakening, the comprehension of the fact that the meaning of life is revealed at the place of the inexistence of all things. But this void is not nothingness. Barking is also a *membrane* that allows self-consciousness to reach the heart of the void that it cleaves. And perhaps the whole universe was created in this way by the first Great Dog, the first Great Barking, the Big Bang or the Big Bark; not so much created as cried out, then, like the primal cry of a newborn who has just burst through the placental membrane.

Perhaps the self is born in the very first hours of the cosmos, with the movement of electrons that already traces out a sort of circle, an atomic interiority. Perhaps the terrestrial crust determines the internal self of the earth; the tension of water the self of oceans; the immune system the biological self of the body; the grammar of the DNA the symbolic self of living systems ... Perhaps the dog is only the latest step in this immense history that overflows every individual being – and to which we, in our turn, must *bear witness*, as the dogs bore witness to Moses during the flight from Egypt.

In fact dogs count on us – as do all animals – to perpetuate their history. All animals, not just dogs, have their eyes on us; all animals participate in this doggish joy. Great apes can be merry, birds can be cheeky, horses grateful. Who knows whether even insects may be capable of kindness? They all know a little of what dogs know, they just display it less overtly. In 'animal' there is *anima*, the soul, the spirit. Animals, then – dogs, but also plants, and perhaps even rocks – leave it to us to fulfil the destiny of the earth, to maintain the cycle of the seasons, to watch over the balance between life and death – in short, to protect the mysteries of Eleusis and Easter, which have never been anything but the mysteries of life. And if there is one thing liable to dampen the great joy of all these animals, it is this and this alone: that we should prove incapable of living up to their expectations. If we have a duty towards the beasts, it is ultimately this: not necessarily to protect them from suffering – for, alas, it is not within our power to prevent life from being a 'Golgotha of the Spirit' (Hegel) – but simply not to betray the hope they have placed in us.

GABRIEL

Clifford Simak's anticipatory novel *City* is profoundly marked by the pessimism of its times with regard to human nature. And perhaps we do have to resign ourselves to the idea that humanity has failed at its task – ultimately the only one that is incumbent upon it. Perhaps we have betrayed the dogs, since we have failed the earth. But then, who can do better than us?

Whatever Simak may think, I don't believe that dogs will save us a second time. Yet we may save ourselves by becoming dogs – and this is perhaps the deeper meaning of his vision according to which the future belongs to the dogs. If we could become dog midwives of a creature capable of taking over from us, then yes, history would continue. The animals would not have died in vain. We would have been worth giving birth to, and we would have compensated them for all of the suffering it took to conceive us.

In 1954 Salvador Dalí painted himself in *Dali, Nude, Entranced in the Contemplation of Five Regular Bodies Metamorphosed in Corpuscles, in Which Suddenly Appears Leonardo's Leda, Chromosomatised by the Face of Gala* (in his own inimitable words). Stretched out in the lower right-hand corner of this painting, which depicts a sort of cosmic visitation, is a patchy dog that Dalí had already painted some years earlier, and that represents him in the foetal state, contemplative, pre-sexuate. This dog is the 'cosmic child' we must learn how to be today, if we wish to fulfil our contract with nature.

Ghost in the Shell, a manga film that portrays how humans are surpassed by an artificial intelligence, also features a cosmic dog that appears fleetingly a number of times. This is Gabriel, the Basset Hound that belongs to director Mamoru Oshii, who wanted to use him as a way to signify that the dog has a role to play in the process of our evolution. Its role is easy to comprehend: to allow a new self to be born.

Research in artificial intelligence has made great progress, and yet it always runs up against the problem of consciousness. No one has yet succeeded in making a computer really intelligent. No one has yet succeeded in writing the line of code that would finally lead to the miraculous awakening of the machine. Gabriel reminds us that the reason for this is that consciousness is not an algorithm more highly developed than others, it is not the icing on the cake of intelligence, it is not even a higher function of the brain. Consciousness is the body of the spirit, its membrane, its dog, its womb. Desire, not intelligence: this is indeed the key to the riddle set by the Sphinx, which Oedipus solved for us. The human being is the animal that has desire, the animal kept upright by invisible wings.

I believe the first artificial intelligence will be produced by a dog, or more exactly by a human artful enough to think like a dog, who will therefore have understood that consciousness has to be included in the very construction of his or her programme, and that it must be so included in the form of a membrane, an immune system that protects the code and by the same token allows the machine finally to be turned on and to stand up on its own.

Epilogue

There is another dog hidden in the Bible, but it is so small and its appearance so fleeting that it is easy to miss. It appears in the sixth chapter of the Book of Tobias, when Raphael appears to Tobias to lead him towards an ointment that should cure his father's blindness. Here, appearing out of nowhere, there is a dog: 'And Tobias went forward, and the dog followed him', says the text laconically.

In a painting inspired by this scene, Verrocchio delivers what is perhaps the key to this 'apparition' by bizarrely inverting the order of things: the dog is *in front of* the angel, the child behind, following. What is more, the dog (a white poodle) is almost transparent. We can see the landscape distinctly through its coat. It is the dog that has a literally angelic body. It looks like a cloud, like Snoopy with his round, vaporous forms, perhaps the only dog that an artist has ever truly succeeded in representing.

In Greek mythology – once again – we find that the word that has come down to us as 'angel' (ἄγγελος, 'messenger' in ancient Greek) appears in the name of a woman, Angelia. Driven from Olympus by her mother Hera, queen of the gods, she was forced to seek refuge in the chamber of a woman who was giving birth, and then in that of a dead person being embalmed. Finally she was purified in a river, the Acheron, from which she was reborn to become the assistant of the queen of the underworld, a queen who, herself, is already many, alternating between Artemis, Hecate, and Persephone. In other words, in the figure of Angelia all aspects of the dog come together once more: protector of pregnant women, embalmer of the dead, crosser of rivers, fertiliser of humans. How could we not see that the angel who guides Tobias and Raphael is Angelia, the little poodle that follows them but that Verrocchio quite rightly placed *before* them, and that all dogs are angels, or that all angels, with their indefinable sex, are Sphinxes, flying phalluses, and that this is indeed why they have no sex – because they *are* one?

To have a dog is to have an angel by your side. Mine was a Basset Hound. He possessed the grave and profound joy of Droopy and a body heavy and dense with the earth's divinities, like Gabriel. I went to look for him in the mountains of the French countryside because I had seen on the Internet that a dog curiously named Martin Luther had been born there. I wanted to see this as a sign, and I was not wrong. His short lifetime was a turning point in my own life. For he opened the doors of nature to me, a nature that, as an impoverished materialist, I had opposed to spirit; but he also opened up the spirit, which, as an impoverished intellectual, I had not understood as desire. He opened me up to the *full* meaning of the mystery of the unity of thought and being that is the other name of the Eleusinian mysteries. He shared with me the secret of his joy and wisdom, so much so that I now realise that I need not be afraid of the new angels that it falls on us, in our turn, to be.

'A painting by Klee called *Angelus Novus*', wrote Walter Benjamin in 'Theses on the Philosophy of History', represents an angel that seems on the point of running from something that he is watching. His eyes are open wide, his mouth gaping, his wings out. This is what the Angel of History looks like. Its face is turned toward the past. Where we see a chain of events, he only sees one unique catastrophe, which ceaselessly heaps up ruin upon ruin and throws them at our feet. Of course he wants to slow down, to bring back the dead and put back together what has been broken. But from Paradise there blows a tempest that is taken in his wings, so violently that the angel can no longer close them again. This tempest pushes him irresistibly toward the future which he turns his back on, whereas the heap of ruins before him raises to the sky. This tempest is what we call progress.

To which I would add: this angel also – this angel above all – is a dog, one of those that run excitedly ahead of their master, constantly looking over their shoulder to make sure the walking catastrophe that we are is still following along behind.

Thy Master, a Dog.

References

Dogs in literature

Investigations of a Dog, in *The Great Wall of China: Stories and Reflections*
by Franz Kafka (trans. Willa and Edwin Muir)
Martin Secker, 1933

Thy Servant a Dog
by Rudyard Kipling
Macmillan, 1930

City
by Clifford Simak
Four Square, 1965

West of Rome
by John Fante
Black Sparrow Press, 1986

Afterglow (A Dog Memoir)
by Eileen Myles
Grove Atlantic, 2017

Dogs in science

The Truth about Dogs: An Inquiry into the Ancestry, Social Conventions, Mental Habits, and Moral Fiber of Canis Familiaris
by Stephen Budiansky
Viking, 2000

Animals in Translation: Using the Mysteries of Autism to Decode Animal Behavior
by Temple Grandin and Catherine Johnson
Scribner Book Company, 2004

The First Domestication: How Wolves and Humans Coevolved
by Raymond Pierotti and Brandy R. Fogg
Yale University Press, 2018

The Invaders: How Humans and their Dogs drove Neanderthals to Extinction
by Pat Shipman
Harvard University Press, 2015

Dogs in mythology
The Wolfman and Other Cases
by Sigmund Freud

The Companion Species Manifesto
by Donna Haraway
Chicago University Press, 2003

Dogs in philosophy

Difficult Freedom, Essays on Judaism
by Emmanuel Levinas

L'atelier d'Alberto Giacometti
by Jean Genet
Editions L'Arbalète, 1963

Dogs in art

Pierre Huyghe: On Site
by Marie-France Rafael
Verlag der Buchhandlung Walther Konig, 2013

William Wegman: Being Human
by William A. Ewing (Author), William Wegman (Photographer)
Thames and Hudson, 2017

Medieval Dogs
by Kathleen Walker-Meikle
The British Library Publishing Division, 2013

Index of dogs

INDEX OF DOGS

INDEX OF PEOPLE

INDEX OF PEOPLE